A Short History of
Mission San Miguel

Ryan Thornton, OFM

A Short History of San Miguel Mission
Ryan Thornton, OFM

For information regarding permission, write to:
Tau Publishing,
Attention: Permissions Dept.
1422 East Edgemont Avenue
Phoenix, AZ 85006

First Edition, June 2011
10 9 8 7 6 5 4 3 2 1

ISBN: 978-1-935257-87-5

Published by Tau Publishing, LLC, Phoenix, AZ

Tau-Publishing.com
Words and Works of Inspiration

TABLE OF CONTENTS

THE PEOPLE AND THE PADRES............. 1

FOUNDING FRIARS……………………………………….. 1

THE PEOPLE………………………………………………… 2

AND THE REST……………………………………………… 6

FRAY LOCO…………………………………………………. 6

MISSION DAYS………………………………… 7

WHODUNIT? POISONING AT THE MISSION…………..... 8

SECULARIZATION……………………………………….. 11

MURDER AT THE MISSION………………………………… 18

DESPERADO DAYS………………………….. 26

RE-BEGINNING………………………………… 28

RENEWAL AND REBUILDING: 1878-1928…………… 28

RENAISSANCE AND RECONSTRUCTION: 1928-1968… 30

A REST: 1968-2003……………………………………... 35

RESTORING AND REOPENING: 2003-PRESENT……… 36

If you were to write a history about your house, what would you say? Would you start with the facts—when it was built, what it is made out of, or how big it is? Or would you tell some stories about it—who was there, how they lived, or what happened?

The truth is that you would probably want to do both: you would want to tell others about where it was and what it looked like, that is the facts, and you would want to tell them about what happened there and how it happened, that is the story. A good history will describe the details and the drama of a thing, whether that thing is your house, your town, or a Mission.

All that is what this little book tries to do. It tries to tell you the who, what, and how of Mission San Miguel Arcángel in a way that will capture your imagination. Every place has its story, and the story of Mission San Miguel is as interesting and exciting as any other out there.

And the hope is that after reading this you will not only know the facts about the Mission, but you will also understand the spirit and significance of Mission San Miguel because then its story will become part of your own story.

The People and The Padres

Founding Friars

Mission San Miguel was founded on July 25th, 1797 by Fr. Fermín Francisco de Lasuén, the successor to

Blessed Junípero Serra as Presidente of the Missions of Alta California. He founded it on the way down from founding Mission San Juan Bautista, making it the 16th Mission in Alta California.

Some people say that the 16 columns along the front wing are in honor of the fact that it was the 16th Mission. Unfortunately, the 3 columns nearest the church are not original. This means that the number is merely coincidental.

More importantly, Mission San Miguel has the distinction of being one of the few missions to be founded at the request of the Native Americans themselves. The Native Americans had seen how nearby Mission San Antonio had benefited the people there with improved agricultural methods as well as education, and they wanted this lifestyle too. 15 children were baptized on the day of the Mission's founding at their parents' insistence. In fact, this community of Native Americans would be the backbone of Mission San Miguel until the destruction caused by the Mexican government.

The People

The Native Americans who asked that Mission San Miguel be built were members of the tribe now known as "Salinan," taking their name from the nearby Salinas River. The Salinans quickly began to identify the Mission as the symbol of their society. For example, the language that the Salinans spoke in that area was named after Mission San Miguel.

Over the altar in the Mission church appears the All-Seeing Eye of God. A traditional symbol among the local Salinans who requested the building of the Mission, it represents God always watching out over and protecting the world.

Additionally, the community of Salinans who lived and worked at the Mission, called neophytes because they were *new* to the Christian *faith*, grew rapidly from the founding of the Mission onward. Their number peaked at 1,076 in 1814. During this time, they worked

3

hard, and the Mission prospered. In fact, they built the current church in just two years (1816-1818) and painted it in three (1818-1821) while under the direction of the Spanish artist Estevan Munras. The murals on the walls of the Mission church are very significant because they are the only original paintings done by Native Americans that are left in any of the California Missions. They are the same as they were in 1821 and real treasures of history and culture. They are also why some call Mission San Miguel the most historic of all the California Missions.

The relationship between the Salinans and the Franciscan padres was very good. A perfect symbol of this is the large window of the church that faces east. Each year on October 4th the friars celebrate the feast of their founder, Saint Francis of Assisi. And as the sun rises on that day each year, this window forms a perfect square of light around the statue of St. Francis on the left side of the altar. This very special effect is called a Mission Illumination. While artistically it is very remarkable, it is also very important culturally.

At the time of the church's construction, the padres were still new to that area and did not know where the sun rose at various times of the year. This means that they could not have positioned the window properly on their own to achieve this effect. Likewise, the Salinans had never made two-storey buildings before and did not have the architectural knowledge to build a window like this either. And so, both the padres and the Salinans had to work together in order to create a window in the church that could illuminate a statue at the other end of the building at a very specific time in the year. It is a perfect symbol of how both the padres and the Salinans worked together to achieve something very good and very beautiful at Mission San Miguel.

A classic example of Mission Illumination, a box of light surrounds the statue of Saint Francis of Assisi in the Mission church every year on October 4th.

And The Rest

There were also some soldiers stationed at Mission San Miguel, who acted like police officers at the Mission to protect all who lived there, both padres and Native Americans. Their part in the history of the Mission is a rather small one, though. It seems as if Mission San Miguel was a quiet post, since the canon brought with the first four soldiers was unearthed in the 1890s after being buried in dirt because it was never used. It was cast in 1697 and fired for the 4th of July celebrations in 1896. Other than this, its history in the past century primarily consists of appearing in different locations around the Mission and being photographed.

Fray Loco

Many Franciscans who have lived at Mission San Miguel thought they were about to go insane. It turns out that the first one did. At its founding, two missionaries were named to serve: Fr. Buenaventura Sitjar of nearby Mission San Antonio and Fr. Antonio de la Concepción Horra, a newcomer. The founding was on July 25th; by August 19th, Fr. Sitjar had to go to the Presidente of the Missions, Fr. Lasuén, in Santa Barbara to tell him personally about Fr. Horra's state.

There are a number of accounts of Fr. Horra's actions, all of them quite bizarre. First, he hid pistols

6

inside of his habit, that is his robes, and walked around with a "swagger." Second, he would make the soldiers and Native Americans perform target practice in front of each other, the first with guns and the others with bows and arrows. He might sound a bit like a cowboy, which, however exciting, was "not in keeping with his calling," to quote Fr. Lasuén.

Unsurprisingly, the Presidente sent another friar to take Fr. Horra away to Monterey "by gentle means…or any way he can." There he was pronounced insane and sent back to Mexico. Almost everyone agrees that the cause of his insanity was the heat of San Miguel, described famously in the following manner, "The fleas cannot endure the summer months, and during the heat of the day may be seen gasping upon the brick pavements." And considering the fact that Fr. Horra's first (and only) month was August, anyone who has lived in San Miguel can only imagine what it must have been like to be there without much water or shade or a house in which to sleep. In short, it would be enough to drive a man mad, which is precisely what it did.

Mission Days

Nothing was, nor even will be, perfect at Mission San Miguel. The first mission bell, like the first missionary, cracked after a very short period of time. Things were going quite well when five padres were poisoned and a fire destroyed two buildings, all of their contents, as well as part of the church. Then, on top of it all, the Mexican government started to meddle in Mission matters. This was all part of life in the so-called "Mission Days" of San Miguel.

In 1806 a fire destroyed part of the church at Mission San Miguel, and a new church was built next to its eastern wall. In this 1870s photo both the current Mission church and the walls of the previous church can be seen.

Whodunit? Poisoning at the Mission

In December of 1800, the two friars stationed at Mission San Miguel, Fr. Juan Martín and Fr. Baltasar Carnicer, fell ill with severe stomach pains, followed by "convulsions and spasms." A third friar, Fr. Marcelino Ciprés, came from Mission San Antonio in order to attend to them. After sending a letter to the Presidente of the Missions, he too was stricken with the illness.

The Presidente had already given orders to remove Fr. Carnicer and Fr. Martín when the news came that Fr. Ciprés had been rushed back to Mission San Antonio after falling ill as well. Mission San Miguel was now without any friars, so the Presidente dispatched Fr. Francisco Puyol on Christmas Day to Mission San Antonio and then to Mission San Miguel in order to give aid. Meanwhile, word came of a rumor that foul play was involved, so the Presidente sent Fr. Pedro Martinez to meet up and join Fr. Pujol at Mission San Miguel as well.

By February of 1801, three Native Americans were suspected of having poisoned the three padres since they had boasted about doing it. They were arrested and brought to the presidio or government headquarters in Monterey for trial. But then Fr. Pujol, now at Mission San Miguel, fell ill with the same sickness at the end of February. Soon after, he was moved to Mission San Antonio, but it was too late. Two weeks later, after suffering "horrible pains," he died. The surgeon performed an autopsy and declared that he had been poisoned.

This threw everything into disarray. During his sickness, Fr. Martín had refused to believe he was poisoned, but after returning to Mission San Miguel and seeing what happened to Fr. Pujol, he had no doubt that he was poisoned by the Native Americans. Fr. Carnicer was about to return as well, but he arrived at Mission San Antonio just in time to see Fr. Pujol dying. The result was that he refused to go back to Mission San Miguel and went to Monterey instead. And then Fr. Martinez started to exhibit symptoms of the illness, too. There was so much confusion and fear that the Presidente was ready to go to Mission San Miguel himself to investigate.

Instead, the Spanish government sent a commission from Monterey to look into the matter at Mission San Miguel, and they ordered the three Native American suspects held in Monterey to be brought down. While under guard at Mission Soledad, the three suspects escaped, apparently because their guard was drunk. The guards tried to pursue them, but were unable to follow the tracks. However, it turned out that two of the suspects actually fled to Mission San Miguel and attempted to find refuge in the church. More soldiers were sent from Monterey, and they managed to apprehend the third suspect en route.

As if a comedy of errors, the commission of inquiry had just returned to Monterey when news of the suspects' capture reached them, so they immediately left for Mission San Miguel again. But the question remained: who did it?

There are two clues. First, as discussed, the Native Americans of Mission San Miguel were not violent, nor did they have resentments towards the friars; such an act would have been both uncharacteristic and unmotivated. Furthermore, the fact that two of the suspects actually fled to the Mission church after their escape would have been inexplicable if they were guilty. Secondly, the poisonings continued well after the three Native Americans were arrested, which meant that the poison was not given directly, but was still somewhere at the Mission. And that is how the mystery would be solved. The answer is: the friars did it.

As was logical, someone eventually examined the padres' living quarters and made a crucial discovery. The padres liked to drink something called mescal, which is like tequila, and they stored it in a copper container. Although the container was lined with tin, the copper went through the tin and tainted the liquor so that "it looked like whey," or watery milk.

In light of the evidence, the friars hurried to affirm the innocence of the accused, particularly since they were the true culprits. By May 28th, 1802, the case had all but been dismissed: the sentence was a flogging in addition to time served, mostly because the suspects boasted of having poisoned the padres.

Secularization

Mission San Miguel was to suffer the same fate as all the missions of Alta California—"secularization." The theory of secularization was sound: over time, the missions should function solely as churches and the land should be given to the people who work it. However, the practice of secularization in Alta California was catastrophic: it demoralized and dispersed the Native Americans and made the missions into museums at best, motels at worst. There is no better case than that of Mission San Miguel to show that the government betrayed the real interest of the governed to the economic interests of the governing.

After gaining independence from Spain in 1821, Mexico began to promote secularization as government

Two of the oldest artifacts at Mission San Miguel are this Spanish bell and cannon. The bell has been in use since 1800, while the cannon was brought at the Mission's founding in 1797.

policy. In 1828, the Mexican governor of California published a plan for the secularization of the missions, which became law in 1830. The law required a special commissioner to go to each mission in order to inform the Native Americans that the mission lands would be given to them and they would no longer be bound to the missionaries (just to the government), as long as they accepted the proposal.

Juan Bautista Alvarado, a future governor of California, was sent from Monterey to Mission San Miguel for this very purpose. In his memoirs, Alvarado writes about what happened when he came to the Mission. He first went to the head missionary, Fr. Juan Cabot, who suggested that Alvarado explain his plan to all the Native Americans at once. The version of the story that follows is in Alvarado's own words:

> In no time, the courtyard of the ex-mission was full of neophytes, and I set out the purpose of my mission and the advantage that it would provide for them and their descendants if they adopted the proposed plan of colonization. The neophytes did not say a single word during the whole time that I, having mounted an open cart, was advising them to give their approval to my plan which contained in it a brilliant future for their race, then so oppressed and—in opposition to the laws of Mexico—deprived of their right to reside where it was more to their liking and to

serve — if they should serve — people more likely to benefit them.

As I concluded speaking, I said, "All the neophytes who want to continue living with Padre Cabot, go to my left; and those who prefer to become land owners and free men, go to my right." And even though it embarrasses me to write this, it falls to me to report that many hundreds of Indians went to my left and shouted, "We want to stay with the padre, he is very good, and we love him!" Some thirty or forty went to my right, but as they saw that they were in an insignificant minority, they also went to the other side and left me alone — totally alone! That occasion made me think of the old Roman woman who began to cry when she learned of the death of Nero: she said that a known evil is better than an unknown good. Without doubt, the natural instinct of the Indians induced them to think in the same way. Perhaps, they made a mistake? I appeal to the result, and each one of my readers may judge what seems better to them.

As is obvious in the case of Mission San Miguel, secularization never had the support of the people who actually lived at the Missions. Nevertheless, the central government of Mexico overrode the popular vote. Under pressure from Mexican businessmen who wanted the Mission lands for themselves, the Mexican Congress declared that "the government shall proceed to secularize the missions of Upper and Lower California."

This law required that the Franciscan missionary be removed, a new priest be appointed to handle the spiritual affairs of the mission, and a government administrator be put in charge of the mission's property. What this meant was that the Native Americans would have to work more in order to provide money for both a priest and an administrator. (Previously the friar or Franciscan missionary received no money, but lived off of what was produced on the lands.) On August 9, 1834, Mission San Miguel became the property of the Mexican government.

First, it took two years for the government to appoint an administrator to Mission San Miguel. The confiscation combined with the absence of an administrator left the Mission in a state of limbo. While the Franciscan missionary was allowed to stay, he no longer had any authority over the land and was limited to spiritual affairs. The result of this was devastating: one writer declared that in the time between her visit in 1833 and her return in 1835, "All of the assets of the Mission, herds, etc., had disappeared." Her assessment does not seem off; between the Annual Report of 1832 and the government's 1839 inventory, the livestock alone had been reduced by 60%. Additionally, between 1837 and 1839 the government's own assessment of Mission San Miguel reduced its value from $82,806 to $74,763, a 10% decrease.

It was obvious, even to the government, that there was a problem. As a result, the same Alvarado, now governor of California, appointed William Hartnell as Inspector of the Missions. Arriving at Mission San Miguel in the summer of 1839, he made the following note in his journal dated August 3rd: "[The Indians] ask that the administrator be removed; they want to be alone with the father." Once again, the desire of the Native Americans to live and remain with their padre went unheeded by the government.

Regardless of the intent of the government, the actual result of secularization was the moral, economic, and cultural devastation of the Missions. Still, this was not enough for the government. On May 28, 1845 the

Secularization was a catastrophe for Mission San Miguel by almost every measure. Over time, the mission fell into a significant state of disrepair as seen in this 1908 photo.

new governor, Pio Pico, decreed that the Native Americans of Mission San Miguel and four others must return to their Missions within a month; if they did not, these Missions would be declared ownerless. At this point, there was no one left to either hear about the law or to follow it. As a result, on October 28, 1845 Pico signed the law that decreed the sale of the Missions to private individuals. Mission San Miguel was the last Mission to be sold on July 4, 1846, three days before Monterey was captured by the United States in the Mexican-American War.

This story sounds like a tragedy. There are victims and villains, plots and protagonists, even a possible happy ending that comes just a moment too late. It is a drama, to be sure. Still, there are some other aspects of all this that ought to be shared. Despite the government's interference, the Franciscan padres from first until last refused to take a salary from the Native Americans; they were content solely with the surplus that was produced from the land. In the case of Fr. Cabot mentioned above, he was so poor at the end of his 21 years of service at Mission San Miguel that he could not afford to return to his native Spain in order to retire. He was the first missionary when the government arrived; the last was no different.

Fr. Ramon Abella was the last Franciscan appointed to San Miguel during the Mission Days, his tenure lasting from 1840 until 1841 when he was moved to Mission San Luis Obispo for reasons of health. At the time of his death, the French writer Eugene Duflot de Mofras saw and described him in this way: "this poor Franciscan sleeps on a hide, drinks from a horn, and eats only meager strips of jerked beef. The venerable Father distributes the little that is sent him among the Indian children, who with their parents occupy the tumble-down houses that surround the Mission."

Such were the men that time and again the Native Americans preferred to all the promises of the government. Much has been said about this moment in the history of Mission San Miguel, because this is the moment when one era began and another ended. It was not progress by any standard, and it was loss by every measure. In short, what was called "secularization" was, in fact, devastation.

Murder at the Mission

Mission San Miguel was sold by the Mexican government to Petronillo Rios and William Reed on July 4, 1846 for $300. While both owners of the Mission, only Reed and his family lived at the Mission, taking up a few of the rooms in the front wing and using the extra ones to provide an inn for travelers. As business partners, Rios and Reed sold supplies to the many prospectors that traveled up the Camino Real at that time to the goldfields of Northern California. They themselves had gone north to try their luck at the gold mines, and even though they were not as successful as Reed had hoped, that did not prevent him from boasting as if they had hit the mother load. As it turns out, it was not the men coming up the Camino Real, but those coming down that would change Mr. Reed's life.

At the end of 1848 five men made their way south from the gold mines of California. They were two Americans, a German, and an Irishman: the German was a deserter from Fort Leavenworth in New York State; the Irishman a desperado, who had murdered a man at Murphy's Camp and escaped from jail. Nothing more is known about the two Americans, because about a day's journey from Mission San Juan Bautista they were killed by the other two who took their gold and split it between themselves. The German's name was Joseph Lynch. The Irishman's name was Pete Raymond, though no one was quite sure because they called him both "Mike" and "Bill." These two continued on to San Juan Bautista, where they purchased two horses and made their way to Mission La Soledad.

There they met five other men, three of whom joined them. Two were deserters from the warship *Warren*, Peter Quin and Peter Remer by name; the other was a mysterious figure called Barnberry, about whom nothing else is known save that his full name was Sam

Bernard. Last, an Indian from the Mission rounded out their lot, called John. It is not difficult to imagine the motives that would have bonded such a band of brothers, such merciless men on that December day in 1848. It may have been fate who was their companion, but fortune was certainly their goddess.

Around three or four o'clock in the afternoon on December 4th, they arrived at Mission San Miguel. As was his custom, Mr. Reed entertained the six men hospitably as lodgers. And as was also his custom, he bragged to them about his own trip to the gold mines and how much he had taken back with him; he even boasted that his little boy could not lift the smallest sack of his gold. The men sold Mr. Reed their gold, paid for their room and board, and spent the night. The next day the group set out, but only went a short ways before discussing Mr. Reed's gold and deciding to return to the Mission. It was December 5th.

When they came back to the Mission, they acted as if they had decided to buy some supplies before continuing onward. Again, Mr. Reed showed them great hospitality. Around seven or eight o'clock that evening, the six men were sitting with Mr. Reed around the fire in the salon, as he continued to entertain them.

The fire was getting low, so Barnberry proceeded to cut some wood into smaller sticks with an axe. Standing behind Mr. Reed, he came forward and threw the sticks onto the fire. As Mr. Reed continued to talk, Barnberry took the axe and struck him several times while the Indian jumped up and stabbed him with a knife. Immediately, the desperados made their way into the kitchen and killed the black cook.

From the kitchen, they went along the back to Mr. Reed's room where the women and children were. For Mrs. Reed was with child and had with her a midwife; the midwife, in turn, had her daughter and her daughter's four year-old with her. Also present in the room were Mrs. Reed's brother, himself just a child, and the five year-old grandson of the Indian sheepherder. And then there was Mr. Reed's little boy, the unfortunate subject in his father's vain boast.

The six men approached the door, and as Mike opened it, he said, "Buenas noches, Señoritas." The desperados showed no mercy and killed the women first. The two little boys were about the same age and, as one might well imagine in such a scene, had tried to hide themselves under the bed. Barnberry and Quin pulled them out from underneath and killed them in cold blood. Some even say that you can still see a gash in the wall from where Barnberry's heavy axe cut straight through the head of the Indian child and hit the wall behind the bed.

At some point in the murderous frenzy, the desperados also killed Mrs. Reed's young brother. But there was yet more murder to come. The men proceeded to a back room in the Mission where the Indian sheepherder was sleeping; Barnberry kicked down the door, and they butchered him as well.

Then the murderers set about to move all the bodies to the carpenter's shop. But as they were moving the bodies from the room where the women and children were, they discovered that Mr. Reed's little boy had hidden out of the way. Barnberry took him in his arms and carried him into the carpenter's shop with all the dead bodies. In perhaps the only moment of true remorse in the whole account, it seems that Barnberry could not bring himself to kill the child, who was a mere infant.

The two wooden crosses in the center of the photograph are the only markers of the gravesite of the 11 people murdered at Mission San Miguel on the night of December 5th, 1848.

It was a scene as poignant as it was barbaric. While the others debated what to do outside, Remer went into the room and soon walked out, saying, "I settled it."

As they were moving the bodies to the carpenter's shop, a mail carrier by the name of Jim Beckwourth was heading north to Monterey and arrived at the Mission. Coming up the main road which was in front of the Mission, he found everything quiet and the front door locked. Walking then through the nearby sheep-gate to the back, he went into the nearest room and found the cook dead on the kitchen floor. He immediately rode to the closest ranch in Paso Robles about five miles away, where he gathered a group and returned to the Mission. When they arrived later that same night, they found that the body of the cook was gone and followed a trail of blood to the carpenter's shop where all the bodies had been piled.

Beckwourth's arrival was unknown to the murderers, apparently because they were in the back in the carpenter's shop at the time. And so, after moving the remaining bodies, they went into Mr. Reed's room and drank some wine. Soon thereafter, they took the axe again and opened up all of Mr. Reed's chests in the Mission, taking what was of value. But they found none of the gold of which Mr. Reed had spoken. Afterwards they immediately began to make their way south, sleeping the rest of the night midway between the Mission and Paso Robles.

On the night of the murders, the mail carrier Beckwourth continued on to Monterey where he informed the authorities there two days after the fact. Had this been the only party to set out after the desperados, they may well have gotten away. However, on the 6th of December, the mayor of San Luis Obispo arrived at the Mission and discovered the bodies as well. He continued on to San Luis Obispo, and the next day sent Trifon Garcia as his representative to apprehend the murderers.

It was then that things started to go badly for the desperados. On the night of the 6th, about five miles south of San Luis Obispo, the Indian deserted them. And it was the following day that Garcia and his men set out after them only five miles away. The desperados outpaced Garcia and his men until December 10th when they camped a mile south of Santa Barbara while the others arrived in the town that same day. Garcia and his group went to the vice-consul of Spain, who organized a posse from Santa Barbara to capture the murderers.

On the 11th of December at about one o'clock, the posse caught up with the desperados at Ortega Hill, about six or seven miles south of Santa Barbara near the present town of Summerland. The posse broke into two lines and yelled "Halt" in both English and Spanish. Two

24

of the desperados, Mike and Barnberry, immediately started shooting and killed one of the posse, named Ramon Rodriguez. A gun fight then broke out; Barnberry was shot and killed, while Mike was mortally wounded and threw himself into the sea. The other three, Lynch, Quin, and Remer, were captured and confessed; they were brought to trial and convicted of the murders on December 26th. On December 28th they were executed by firing squad.

There is yet still an ironic twist to the story. For the fate of the murdered and the murderers' bodies was the same. Lynch, Quin, and Remer were given the last rites of the Catholic Church from one of the few padres left in California, stationed at Mission Santa Barbara. And as such, they were buried on the grounds of that same mission. Mr. Reed's business partner, Petronillo Rios, buried his friend and the other victims of the murder at their home, that is Mission San Miguel. The bodies were placed in two opened tombs, located just "outside the rear door of the sacristy, a little to the southwest and near the old first church wall," forming one mass grave. To this day, the grave remains unmarked, save for an old wooden cross.

Thus, both bodies of murderers and murdered lie in the hallowed grounds of mission cemeteries, warnings and witnesses to what happens in a world that knows only vanity and greed. The same lot, even the same plot, does fall to all.

Desperado Days

Beginning with the murder of the Reed family in 1848, Mission San Miguel entered a thirty-year period best termed as its "Desperado Days." The rushed sale of the Mission by the Mexican government followed by the immediate capture of California by the United States in the Mexican-American War left the legality of the deals in doubt. It was not resolved until 1859 when the sales were declared illegal and the property returned to the Catholic Church by President James Buchanan. Up until that point, the Mission had been in the hands of Petronillo Rios, though reports suggest that it was mostly abandoned except for the desperados who used it as a place to rest as they made their way up and down California during the Gold Rush.

It is perhaps unsurprising then that Mission San Miguel was used for a variety of purposes during this time, including store (1868), saloon (1869), dance-hall (1870s), hotel (1876), and an outlet for the Howe Sowing Machine Company (circa 1860s-1870s). What is surprising, though, is that all these commercial enterprises seem to have been done while the Catholic Church had ownership of the property.

Of its popularity, however, there is no question. From early accounts, we know that Mission San Miguel's position halfway on the only road between Los Angeles and San Francisco made it an ideal stop. Indeed, the saloon became so popular that the tenant needed to build a dance-hall in order to meet "the demand for a place of amusement other than a saloon." It is not certain, but it seems that the dance hall took up several of the forward rooms in the front wing of the Mission nearest to the church. More importantly, the Mission was popular because it attracted people, and it was those people that gave it its distinctive coloring during this time. Who they were and what they were like can be easily imagined; in a word, they were desperados.

This late-19th century photo indicates what Mission San Miguel looked like during its so-called "Desperado Days."

Re-beginning

Renewal and Rebuilding: 1878-1928

Times change, however, and so do places. In 1878, clergy returned to Mission San Miguel, but they, like the people, were different: they were diocesan priests, not Franciscan friars, and their congregation consisted of Mexican and white settlers, not Salinans. The Mission itself had also changed. While the church had been spared from desecration, the buildings had been in continual use with minimal repair in the intervening thirty years. The west wing of the quadrangle was run-down, the south wing was roofless, and only about half of the 1806 church that made up the north wing remained. As for the east or front of the Mission, it was in a dismal state despite being the only habitable building; the roof was in obvious disrepair, walls had been removed in order to make room for a large dance-hall, and livestock had thinned the pillars of the interior colonnade to a precarious degree by scratching their sides against them. Such was the state of Mission San Miguel when it became a functioning parish.

The second diocesan priest assigned was Fr. José Mut, who saved the Mission from literally falling into pieces. The Mission at this time was in obvious ruin, and Fr. Mut raised enough money to replace the rotted roof of the east wing and to recast the broken mission bells into a single, large one. These fundraising efforts were extraordinary, and for his incredible work, Fr. Mut received the honor of being buried in the cemetery of the Mission he worked so hard to improve, the only diocesan priest buried at the Mission and the only priest buried in its cemetery.

While no one would match Fr. Mut's fundraising abilities for over a century, the precedent had been set. His successors worked hard to continue to improve the Mission both spiritually and materially, the chief of whom was Fr. Henry S. O'Reilly. It was Fr. O'Reilly who

This is the earliest known photograph of the interior of the Mission church, dated 1894. The priest in the foreground is Fr. Henry S. O'Reilly, originator of the annual Mission Fiesta.

pioneered the idea of celebrating the Mission's Centennial in 1897, which featured a grand three-day celebration with dances and races, prayers and speeches, not to mention a daily sunrise salute with the old Mission cannon. This event was celebrated on the 28th, 29th, and 30th of September and seems to be the origin of the annual Mission San Miguel Fiesta, held on the closest weekend preceding September 29th, the Feast of Saint Michael the Archangel. Although the first was celebrated in 1897, the second would not be celebrated until 1928, thirty years later and on the occasion of the Franciscans returning to the Mission they founded 131 years before.

Renaissance and Reconstruction: 1928-1968

This was the beginning of the Renaissance of Mission San Miguel. While the years under diocesan priests were essential to the continued existence of the Mission, they were also only concerned with the essentials. Other than the church, the front wing was the last building left. In the intervening years, the south wing had been reduced to its foundation, the north wing had continued to degrade, and the west wing had become a mere frame of a structure. Had these basic renovations not been done, it is unlikely that there would have been anything but a church left, and that only for a time. Thus was Mission San Miguel when the Franciscan friars returned from their exile of 87 years.

Over the years, Mission San Miguel's condition had deteriorated considerably. As can be seen in this 1939 photograph, the amount of restoration work that the Franciscan Friars undertook upon their return was vast.

The Franciscans came at an inauspicious time, but no one told them that. Moreover, the friars who rebuilt the Mission were too many and their work too varied to be named individually; it was a communal effort, and it is the community of Franciscans which must receive credit for it. And credit there is. The friars returned on August 1st, 1928, and their first two decades back were marked by the Great Depression and World War II. Yet in this time of scarcity, the padres completely rebuilt the Mission as we know it today and as it stood at its height during the Mission Days of the early 19th century.

Beginning with a restoration of the front wing, the friars proceeded to rebuild the other three wings, reconstructing the walls from the original foundations. Once these were restored, the central courtyard was formed. The walls were then expanded, and work immediately began on actually rebuilding the south and west wings. Originally, both the south and west wings were used for shops; this purpose was maintained in the case of the west wing, but the south wing was made to house bedrooms for candidates in training as Franciscan brothers. Incredibly, both the south and west wings were each completed in less than two years. And as these two wings were being finished, the friars proceeded to rebuild the old church that had comprised the north

All of Mission San Miguel can be seen in this 1940s aerial photograph. From 1928 to 1939, the Franciscan Friars rebuilt much of the Mission, preserving the original foundations throughout.

32

wing, assisted by the fact that the foundations of the church were still entirely intact. The rebuilding of the church took just over a year, in which time the friars also managed to restore the pillars around the courtyard that had been worn down by the sides of livestock over the decades. All told, by 1939 the original Mission quadrangle had been totally restored; in other words, the padres completely rebuilt Mission San Miguel during the Great Depression.

And even after a decade of unparalleled construction, the padres did not rest. While not as dramatic as the total rebuilding of the Mission quadrangle, many important improvements were made, including an outdoor drainage system, various walls to surround the Mission property, as well as the brick walkways in the front and around the courtyard. It was also during this time that the fountain in the front of the Mission was built; though deliberately antiqued to make it look historic, it is, in fact, not. Finally, the decision was made that Mission San Miguel would become the novitiate or the first year of training for both Franciscan brothers and priests; it was a decision that would shape the nature of Mission San Miguel both for the friars themselves and in general.

Structurally, this decision required the building of more rooms; culturally, this decision meant that Mission San Miguel would be a center of activity. The novitiate annex to the west wing of the Mission was completed in 1948, just as the number of Franciscan novices or young men seeking to become friars substantially increased in the years following World War II. And since there was enough room for all these novices, the question became what to do with them.

The answer devised by the senior friars was simple: work. For the next 20 years, class after class of novices provided a free, renewable source of labor whose job was the continuous construction of the Mission. It was the sweat and labor of dozens of young men, eager to live the Franciscan life, that would perpetuate the Renaissance of Mission San Miguel.

Their projects were various, continuous, and arduous: they built endless walls, a three-tiered bell tower, as well as another novitiate wing. Basically, these two decades saw the enclosure of the Mission as we know it today; virtually every boundary wall was constructed during this period of time and, like the fountain in the front, antiqued to look original. The purpose of this, of course, was activity, not authenticity. And that the Franciscans had. The presence of the novitiate gave Mission San Miguel an energetic feel, full of action and excitement. Things always seemed like they were happening because things constantly were happening. It had a Renaissance spirit, pure and simple.

A Rest: 1968-2003

All this ended in a rather definitive way in 1968 when there were simply no more novices. Like the entire Catholic Church, the Franciscans were trying to understand and implement the decrees of the Second Vatican Council. The Church was in a state of updating itself, and the Franciscans with it. As a result, the decision was made to close the novitiate for a year and eventually move it elsewhere. And so, while the Church renewed itself, the Mission aged.

From the years 1968 to 2003, there is little that can be said about Mission San Miguel other than that the

Today the front wing of Mission San Miguel looks much like it did in this 1924 photo. The walls, fountain, and arches that are seen there now are actually constructions of the 1940s and 1950s.

friars remained there and ministered to the people. The buildings did not change, and no major construction was undertaken; to put it simply, it was 35 years of status quo. The novitiate returned in 1994, but it was not the same: there were fewer men, and now they were men, the average age having shifted from 20 to 30. The extra rooms in the Mission were used for retreats, and the field to the south was used to house some assorted livestock.

In short, time passed, and the buildings aged. Minimal repairs were done, and the Mission lay undisturbed, but deteriorating on a quiet stretch of the 101 Freeway in the middle of Central California. That is, until the morning of December 22nd, 2003.

Restoring and Reopening: 2003-Present

In the years leading up to 2003, Mission San Miguel had received attention at the local, state, and national levels regarding its significant need for repair. Decades of reverberations from the railroad and 101 Freeway on either side plus previous earthquakes had cracked the Mission, particularly the church. There was also considerable damage from termites and poor water drainage, not to mention the sacristy which was tilting so far to the right that the sky could be seen through the 8-inch gaps between the ceiling and the wall. This is how the Mission stood three days before Christmas in 2003.

At 11:15 AM on December 22nd, a 6.5-magnitude quake centered in San Simeon rocked the Central Coast of California. The earthquake seriously damaged the Mission with new cracks appearing and the old ones growing larger. In fact, from the inside it was possible to hear the building creak as it tried to resettle. The County of San Luis Obispo closed the Mission to the public while efforts began to analyze the damage and formulate a strategy to repair it.

These were tough times for the Mission. The first estimate for repairs was around $30 million, though this was only a guess. Additionally, the Franciscan friars had fallen into their own financial problems: in the middle of 2004, they were $50,000 in the red, and by the end of the year owed $100,000 in debts. It was at this point, on January 10th, 2005, that the superiors of the Order and the Diocese of Monterey debated whether to close the Mission totally and remove the Franciscans permanently.

But like each dark period in the history of Mission San Miguel, it preceded a dawn. The project team completely reworked their design and offered an innovative, never-before-used solution, which brought the cost for repairs down to $15 million. In turn, a significant donation to the Friars of Mission San Miguel allowed them to pay their bills and stay. And just as importantly, the parish committed itself to work tirelessly towards rebuilding the Mission. With help from several foundations and an insurance settlement, the 7-phase retrofit of Mission San Miguel began. And on September 22nd, 2009, the Mission church was reopened and dedicated.

However, it was the people that reopened Mission San Miguel with golf tournaments, hundreds of bake sales, and donations from their own wallets. Moreover, the many visitors from many places who donated and gave however much they could to the repair and restoration of the Mission are a major reason why it is still here. Halfway through the 7-phase plan, the Mission church and front museum wing are once again open to the public, though more money is still needed to complete the remaining repairs. But as the reopened Mission church continues to draw more visitors and more parishioners, beginning yet another renewal in the history of Mission San Miguel, it is crucial to note that it is the people who are the major players in this era of the Mission's history. It was the people who first wanted a Mission and then built one, and it will be the people who want to keep the Mission that will rebuild it.

And that is the chapter of this history that remains to be written.